"Kevin Ridgeway is a survivor. As other poets these days (including myself) gather vignettes of streetlife from afar, or still dull their brains with chemicals, or teeter on the middle aged tightrope of moderation making monuments to fading glory days; Kevin Ridgeway white knuckles through these bleak times cracking compassionate visions of contemporary characters popping across the page. This is a dispatch from halfway houses, sober living facilities, the frontlines of America. Here are feverish fractals of elaborate blues in cascading Kerouac long lines, telescoping through tunnels of family memories, collapsing into a fading photoplay like a ghost reporting from a future he sometimes doesn't think he deserves. Somehow his writing is melancholy but funny, grounded but surreal, skillful but fresh. It's something worth living for, worth struggling for, and definitely worth reading and enjoying."

- Westley Heine, author of *Busking Blues, Street Corner Spirits, Cloud Watching in the Inferno*

"Kintsugi is the Japanese art wherein the artisan repairs broken pottery with gold which both strengthens the breaks and fissures, but also transforms those imperfections into unique features of sometimes stunning beauty. Kevin Ridgeway's poems do that too. They insist that we look deeply into the shattered lives, the economic precarity, and the mental and emotional stakes of just trying to get by in this country. Ridgeway writes, "nobody wins here", and these spare, translucent poems speak that truth in every line. They are also veined in gold and that's Ridgeway's art, it's one of reassurance and repair. He's a companion for the long roads, a voice that helps us carry on."

-Kristofer Collins, *The Vesper Room*

"There's a chapter in Ray Chandler's *The Little Sister*, where Marlowe drives forties L.A night rattling off all the falsehood gloss of Los Angeles, it's well fixed demons. Occasionally, while driving, while bearing witness, Marlowe stops ranting, reminding himself he's not human tonight. Now, Ridgeway comes along with his coppertone girls, art deco theaters with dollar dogs and all the ghosts of growing up on the other side of the palm tree. You know the black and white of Bunker Hill with cigarette smoke and desperation rising like Angel's Flight herself. These poems may not be Chandler, but they got a hard won grit, an unsatisfied howling that sits with us in all our broken moments. The times where all we have left is our honesty and just enough of sense of humor to keep us alive. If you live the poem, do yourself a favor, crack this book and hang your heartbreaks together."

-Jason Baldinger, *American Aorta*

DEATH OF THE COPPERTONE GIRL

POEMS BY KEVIN RIDGEWAY

LUCHADOR PRESS

Luchador Press

Big Tuna, Texas

Copyright © Kevin Ridgeway, 2025
First Edition: 1 3 5 7 9 10 8 6 4 2
ISBN: 979-8-89975-011-3
LCCN: 2025938310

Author photo: Kevin Ridgeway

Acknowledgments

Some of these poems previously appeared in *Chiron Review, Nerve Cowboy, River Dog, San Pedro River Review, One Art, Main Street Rag, Hole in the Head Review, Trampoline, Meat for Tea, Seppuku, Red Shift, Misfit Magazine, Tickets to Midnight, Hobo Camp Review, Trailer Park Quarterly, A Thin Slice of Anxiety, Black Coffee Review, Panoply, Rusty Truck, Silver Birch Press, Up the River, MacQueen's Quinterly, Raven Road Review, Bold Monkey, Ghost City Review, Heroin Love Songs, Gasconade Review, Big Hammer* and *Muleskinner Review*, with many thanks.

Table of Contents

For Fred Voss

"I am not a demon. I am a lizard, a shark, a heat-seeking panther. I want to be Bob Denver on acid playing the accordion."

—NICOLAS CAGE

EX-BOY

I would always hide
away from the world
in dreams behind closed
curtains, television
scrambling me
into a box of wild cards.

LAST MAN STANDING

The faded patches on the school green
would always dance with dirt inside
of a heat-born mirage. My classmates
argued over which of their kickball teams
would have to take on the liability
of my inclusion. My father was in prison,
my brother was away at college and
my mother was always working
to pay for both. My best friend
was my elderly great-grandmother
until her dementia helped her forget
who I was until the day she died,
at a time when nobody else wanted
to see her that way. I had no choice
but to light my hope in the flicker
of the same old black and white
movies she loved with dead actors
and dead actresses who all picked me
to watch them alone everyday as
the sun faded into a sleepless night
haunted by the desperate wish
that I would wake up inside
an old silent movie in a daydream
where I would never feel left out,
in a place where they'd beg me
not to leave any of them behind.

THE GHOST OF CAL WORTHINGTON

Everyone used to get
the lyrics to the jingle
in his commercials
for his car dealership wrong:
if you're lookin' for a car, go see Cal!
had been misheard over the years as:
if you're lookin' for a car, pussy cow!
He dressed in a country western outfit
and paraded around the lot
of his main dealership
in televised advertisements
with elephants, orangutans
and giraffes, but never a single
pussy cow, to my dismay.
All of these years later,
I search for any signs
of the exotic and elusive pussy cow
at Worthington Ford in Long Beach,
not a single one to be found, other
than the ghost of Cal Worthington
smoking a cigar with a chimpanzee
in the front seat of an old Ford truck,
both of them singing the song
as intended before they disappear
back into the confusion of the past.

MY PEOPLE

a grave
nobody
visits
the misfits
nobody
talks to
those are
my people
dead
or alive
the
forgotten

WHAT GRANDPA WORE
EVERY CHRISTMAS

He wrote us hundred dollar checks
and sat back in his reclining chair,
attired in combat boots and swim trunks
he was wearing over his boxers while
my mother was there. He cracked
a fake smile at the big and tall shirts
we'd gotten him that he never
bothered to wear after locking himself
inside, where he rocketed into a zone
where he could fly away and forget
about his failures in the past and those
swim trunks expanded as he became
submerged in ocean water as though
he was wearing MC Hammer parachute
pants. He was locked inside the attics
of his haunted mind with tortured
whispers no one could hear but me.

BABY'S FIRST NERVOUS BREAKDOWN

Mom gave birth
to a chainsaw nightmare:
a son who dresses as her
for Halloween,
a son who cleaned the house
in a teenaged manic episode
until it was spic and span
telling her not to make a mess
or she's grounded
a son who complained
she wasn't invested in his future
while he walked four miles
to school every goddamn day
to rescue himself from
breathing in hairball grime
to exhale white trash guilt
in primal screams of shame
against walls where
photographs of family
I never met in this life
all hung dead, an audience
for a kid who locked himself
inside alone long enough
to chop through all the scenery
my stay-at-home television father
influenced me to stage
my amateur hour around

until she found me there
bleeding out lost daydreams
the doctors told her
in the emergency room
that I inherited a shipwreck

SAY CHEESE

We thought we had it going on then.
In photographs developed from disposable
1990s cameras, glazed by tans in a bottle,
our Crystal Clear Pepsi future promising,
now a 1950s-esque laughingstock, subject
to the cruel scrutiny of the current generation
of youngbloods after our seats in the universe.
Old cool is honored in punk and early hip hop—
rock and roll has hipster cancer and is dying fast,
a square gyration of coots standing in the way.
Now we are confused by a digital stream
of everything beyond our wildest daydreams
when we posed in baggy Gap corduroy,
our new CD players skipping the soundtrack
to our long wait for the Beautiful People
to share breaking news we can now click for,
mass expertise fueling the dawn of a new age
of smart-ass our feeble minds could not
comprehend. We didn't realize how silly we
would look, knowing smiles unbathed in an
immortality of gigabytes for kids who think we
are less cool than we thought our parents were.

POEM FOR THE PEOPLE
WHO HAVE NOWHERE TO GO

I always like to jam
with salt of the earth
people, the forgotten
ones who don't have
even a kiddie table
to sit at, people like me
now back here in
the cold turkey shakes
of my withdrawal from
my false sense of family,
people I miss who pray
for me and the day
I will be well enough
to board a bus or a train
or an airplane again
among other discount
souls homesick for
a place none of them
will ever go again.

RECESSED IDENTITIES

We always fought over
who got to be who,
our imaginations taking us
far beyond the long
green schoolyard
in warrior's armor,
ready to take on
anything and anyone
once we compromised
over the many
fictional characters
that helped us get away
from ourselves, because
deep down we knew
we couldn't save the world.

THE FRUSTRATION
OF BEING UNPOPULAR

None of the girls were interested.
None of the guys wanted to hang out.
and no matter how hard I tried,
I was never the lead in the school play,
and was never the best at anything
but being alone in my room, where
I plotted and schemed for a way
to get their attention, and decided
to commit suicide, but I'm not the
best at suicide, either. Classmates
sent me letters, strangers who all
wrote that they didn't know me well
but that I mattered enough to stay alive.
I came to our high school graduation,
where none of them knew what
to say to me. I still felt ignored,
and crazy to them. I entered
the adult world a number who is sick
and chained to a system that barely
protects me from the pain of feeling
alone and broken, but I rebuilt
myself into a machine that spits out
endless words to fight the numbers
in a mind bent climb into the arms
of muses who gift me with the peace
of being nameless in an ugliness I've
wrestled into something beautiful,
and that no one even has to see.

BACKSEAT ENLIGHTENMENT

I had a panic attack in the middle
of my first and last driving lesson
from one of my friends who had me
at the wheel of a battered Jeep going
around a maddening mountain range
through the deep, spirited forests
of our youth and my poor friend
took the keys right out of my hands
as a favor to society for ever having
to worry about a tralalala space cadet
like me killing innocent people in a car
neither one of my parents wanted,
even when it was new. Like
everyone else, they both drove me
to where I needed to go, shaking
their clueless heads when I offered
them unsolicited backseat driving
suggestions or whenever I stepped
on the imaginary brakes that kept me
from ever growing up. But I have
gotten around this world so many
more miles than they ever did,
and all I had to do was turn on
my internal zen compass and
point the way for every motorist
I thumbed a ride from on the path
to becoming a gutter zen master

who fled from an unhip world
in search of a new world born
with a new cool I found out there
on the road in the passenger's seat,
dreaming of a fractured revolution.

THE DAY THE MUSIC DIED

One time back in college,
I started singing a song
I'd written during an acid trip
to my classmate, Shelley, who
told me not to quit my day job.
I told her I didn't have one.
She told me I needed to get one.
I didn't listen to her, but I didn't
listen to myself, either,
because even I can't remember
the words to a failed song
no one will ever hear again.

I WANT TO TRAVEL SOUTH THIS YEAR

She was raised
in the same southern town
I once resided in
back when I was still a drifter.
She described it all
like an unbroken pangea
of ancient mimeographed words.
We were there at the same time,
but we never met beyond
our neighboring poems
in small magazines
below the Mason-Dixon line.
I ran away to Austin
just like she did,
but we never crossed paths
there, either: She was hidden
by a mysterious disease
she succumbed to
before I could embrace her
in the melted humidity
of a southern fried daydream.
I now daydream of gothic muses
like her who watch over me
in the swampy funk
of a strange and endless highway
that crosses through
all the blurry memories
of misadventure in
my long and unquiet mind.

MARRIAGE ON ICE

We exchanged daydreams in a bed tucked
inside a loft as snow fell quietly outside,
Pee-Wee Herman waving at us from a
beat up 1980s Magnavox television screen.
We fucked in between shifts at the pharmacy
across the river from Cornish, where
JD Salinger was hiding, and we searched for
him on days when the roads weren't as icy,
dressed up in our red work smocks,
whizzing past the mountainside ranch
of Charles Bronson, the house that
Death Wish bought, all of these strange
childhood heroes who haunted
the heartbeat of our imagination in
the otherwise gray, cold deadbeat sludge
we trudged through to the comfort of a bed
shared by young lovers who had no idea
where we were going, our hope ignited
into flames that kept us both warm, our
passion for one another frozen in a time
when we battled an unbroken cabin fever.

THAT'LL SHOW 'EM

I dropped out
of college
got married
& got a divorce
from a wife
who said I was
too dramatic.
I moved back in
with my mother,
who suggested
I audition at
the local
community theater.
I scoffed at her,
hid in my room,
& started writing
bad poetry instead.

FEEL GOOD NOW

Is there a dopamine shortage going on
that I am not aware of?
My chemicals aren't mixed the way
I prefer for them to be on
a Saturday afternoon—
even the sunshine isn't working,
let alone the convenience of the digital age,
pleasures gained without rising from my bed.
It's getting more expensive
and time consuming a search
for this elusive release hormone junkies
seek without resorting to the drugs
that always manage to stop working,
and are not to mention rapidly life-damaging—
along with everything else that's just a toxic fix
for a problem I'm too lazy and weak to solve.
In America there is a freedom to go insane,
to run away from the guaranteed pain
inherited by everyone that can breathe in
the fumes of an earth burning into extinction
with precarious desires of a human race who
drinks from cups that are always half empty.

TALKING ABOUT PEOPLE WE KNOW

His new wife is a control freak,
doesn't let him on social media,
which is why I haven't heard from him.
Everyone's kids are so annoying, we agree.
Stephen King was a customer at a diner
a friend worked at, and we both light up
when we remember she said he doesn't
believe in giving tips. Her cousin was
the one who hit Stephen King with his car,
I add. Astonished laughter. One guy
who got a Master's from Columbia is
married to the railroad now, never sleeps
in midnight locomotion. Another is a
licensed therapist who toiled internship
hours at Angola, the prison both Dr John
and Leadbelly warned about in their songs.
We pause inside the walls of Angola for a
sobering moment of haunted silence, all of
those poor, lost, beaten souls we will know
only in the groove of a record or the stories
of our classmate's front line experiences
to end the war on humanity. Another
friend plays in a famous rock band
who all went solo. We both lament
the fact that we did not become rock stars
like him. Steely Dan's *Pearl of the Quarter*
oozes out of the car stereo on the drive back

to my hotel. We talk about how they got
their name from a *Naked Lunch* dildo,
with lyrics fueled by referential intricacies
we both crave by two men we talk about
like we knew them our whole lives, they
were with us and everyone else all along,
playing in the background while we would
all talk at after parties on long dormitory
nights about how we wanted to do things
that would leave the world speechless.

JACKPOT ROMANCE

On our walk home one night,
my girlfriend and I found a mountain
of discarded spare change at the bus stop
in front of a closed down Jack in the Box
in West Covina, CA, where we were
both trying to defeat the bottle
by wandering around on buses
and crashing cultural events
at the nearby colleges followed
by midnight movies with the rats
at a sleazy dollar movie theater
in nearby Pasadena whose
dollar hot dogs we lived on
because we were both on disability.
We fell on bruised, flophouse knees
pouring coins into our shopping bags,
both of us astonished at the hard luck break.
We treated ourselves to a late dinner
under the hazy mechanized fluorescent suns
lighting a taco wagon where they wrapped
burritos thicker than my already bulging
beer gut waist line, a minor victory during
our struggle to find light in the darkest places.
But that was years ago, and since then
she lost her battle with the toxic spirits
that have left me dry, slim and with money
in my pocket and a mind that battles

regret for the tragedy of our love
and the end of her life against those
moments when we didn't feel any pain
like we did when we found that mountain
of spare change, which made us feel like
we could afford to love each other forever.

THE KINDNESS OF STRANGERS

We emptied the old house of everything
it collected over sixty years in our family
and everyone gathered to say goodbye
in the front entrance. None of them
noticed I was gone. A tall, leggy beauty
who flipped houses on the real estate
market was *oooo-ing* and *ahhhh-ing*
as I used my once useless
and extensive knowledge
of our family's history
on the tour I charmed her on.
My vivid stories impressed her
before she handed over her business card.
I said goodbye to the old house by reciting
all of my crooked nicotine stained
wallpaper memories to a stranger
before we locked its doors a final time
and I didn't look back when
I followed her shapely ass through
the front door and out of the past.

MOM NEVER GOT A BOOB JOB

She always said she was going
to sue her employer for screwing
her over and use her settlement
to get herself a boob job,
but the money from that lawsuit
is now my inheritance in the wake
of her demise, and I'm using
that money to get myself a boob job.

DETOX 2012

Let It Bleed played
on the car stereo
while I gave her
a squeeze on the wrist.

It was all going to be alright,
but little did we know.

THE DEATH OF THE COPPERTONE GIRL

The billboard
stood above
interstate 5, and
it featured a pretty
cartoon girl with
her bikini bottoms
tugged down
in a mechanical
tug of war
with a cartoon dog,
which showed
off the tan line
of her pale derriere.
She lost one of her legs
during a storm that
left the dog decapitated.
They both stood there
until the bitter end,
when they disappeared
and the sign turned
into a large ad that read:
SHOP AT WAL-MART
and I grieved the loss
of the first woman
I fell in love with
and could not save.

HOLY NIGHT

she spoke of her
dead father to me
while I sat in the
backseat of an Uber
and I looked out
at the dark Christmas Eve
cemetery buried in snow
hundreds of little crosses
marking dead babies
across the highway
from a Savers thrift store
the same chain my
dead mother dragged me
into to go Christmas
shopping and I say
a solemn prayer for
her father, those babies,
my mother, and us.

TRUE LONELINESS

is watching other people bond
and form meaningful relationships
while I sit here talking to myself
until I have developed a cognitive fantasy
juicy enough to transport me from a world
filled with people who all consider me
less important to them than I was to
my dead mom and my dead girlfriend.
I was left with not a cheerleader in sight
now that I've driven all of their love away,
blinded by a trauma that helps me forget
what makes me want to stay here, even
when no one will talk to me but my Dad
in collect calls from prison, when we
commiserate over his dead wife
and my dead girlfriend and how neither
one of us deserved the love taken away
from us by a universe where I float
into black holes in search of any of the love
they might have left behind here in this
long, uncertain darkness to fuel a hope
I'll wake up in the arms of another woman
I've fooled into thinking she loves me.

POEM IN WHICH
MY DEAD GIRLFRIEND
GIVES ME SHIT

I answered her silent questions to me
as I stormed up Pacific Avenue to
the post office, sending off late books
and other unfinished business she began
to haunt me over after my latest
short-lived romance fizzled. She said
I broke one cardinal rule she used to
have for me: *"Don't fuck up."*
I stood there washing my clothes
at the laundromat in a depressive effort
to love myself because she couldn't
anymore, and neither can all the people
who are still alive if I push them away
by behaving like a recovering primadonna
who had relapsed, a spotlight bathed on
the crown of shit I made and wore
upon my crazy head for all the confused,
angry and brokenhearted people to see.

HAUNT

I dined in a booth adjacent to the one we used to share, and two dark-skinned Indian girls dined on Burrito Supremes. I wandered through the parking lot to a downtown intersection, lost in a daze when a homeless man asked me if I needed anything after I gave him a cigarette. I lied when I told him no.

DEAD MOTHER MATHLETE

she talks to me in numbers:
the number 17 greets me everywhere--
same number as the street she used
to work on, and the number 54 won't
leave me alone--half her birth year,
and everywhere I go, I see these numbers
and I say "hi Mom" dozens of times a day
with my apologies to her seething ghost
for always being so terrible at math.

WORRY LINES

I discovered them
on my forehead in the mirror
consequences of brooding
over so many wrinkles in time
now everyone can see
how heavy it is to carry around
a mind like the one I've got
battle scars that begin to show
my entire story without me
having to say a word.

COST OF LIVING

wars
tornadoes
hurricanes
earthquakes
cancer
viruses
mental illness:
we all have
our own
disasters,
buried
in the debt
of fate

MIDNIGHT FUCKHEAD

I wanted to kill the asshole
dressed like a tweaker variation
of Christian Slater's onscreen
impersonation of Jack Nicholson
behind sunglasses for telling me
not to deny I was playing under
the covers with my dick over
the knockers on the crazy girl
outside in the common area
of the local mental hospital. I
screamed and ran out of the room.
They moved me to a room with an
old man with dementia who burst into
tears as he looked out our window
and couldn't even remember the last
son of a bitch who pissed him off.

PURPLE CRAYONS FOREVER

When they gave me
my contraband back
it had half a purple crayon in there
I got home
and changed shirts
felt something
in the front pocket
it was the other half
of the purple crayon

WHAT'S IN A NAME?

Perhaps my missing teeth
give me a speech impediment,
but people assure me
that's it's not an issue,
and they can hear me clearly,
which leaves me wondering
why the cashier at Wendy's
who took my overpriced
double cheeseburger order
got my name so horribly wrong.
I study it there on my receipt
as it laughs, blemished
in awkward embarrassment
for not spelling out "Kevin"
but "Cabin" instead. This
happens to lots of people,
as I've seen from time to time,
but what kind of a name is Cabin?
I can understand maybe Corbin,
as in the actor Corbin Bernsen
(is he dead? ok, maybe I digress)
Friends suggest Cabin might
make a good nickname for me,
or better yet a fictional persona
ala Hank Chinaski or Kilgore Trout.
Cabin Weaver— a poor lost soul
who could barely afford

the lamp warmed beef sandwich
he chews on while high schoolers
laugh amongst themselves,
making old Cabin believe
they're all in on the joke,
birth given to a new pariah
for strange and twisted times,
regardless of what you call him.

THE MAN WHO SLEEPS IN THE BED
NEXT TO ME

My roommate looks like a wrinkled,
glazed-over Stimpson J. Cat at dusk
but transforms into a hyper confident,
thieving upright Yogi Bear at dawn
when I let him bum a cigarette. He
lights it, jabbering my ears off about
how cool it would be if they blasted
Snoop Dog at Knott's Berry Farm
and the time he made out with a girl
in one of the caves on Disneyland's
Tom Sawyer's Island behind a nighttime
performance of Fantasia, when they
witnessed a stabbing while scaling
a phony cavern. He tells me he caught
the guy who did it, and Mickey Mouse
presented him with a cartoon Excalibur.
He tells me the television is talking
to him, and that's the only word of his
that I believe at this point. I wonder
what my roommate dreams about,
it must be better than anything old
Walt could produce on an acid trip.
He's a dog on its birthday that doesn't
know it's his birthday, but I do. I don
his head with a party hat while he tries
to gnaw at it and I snap a photograph
before giving him another special treat.

LOW PATIENT CENSUS

There's no one yelling,
no meltdowns, no crisis—
in fact, the entire back patio
of my treatment center
is encased in holy silence:
only ghosts of patients past
and me, serene enough
to walk out of here,
but this is my headcase
sanctuary. Strands of smoke
from my cigarette rotate
into warped mandalas
rising out over the fence
into the adjacent alleyway
where nirvana is interrupted
by a homeless man's
dirty chain-linked fence
request for a spare smoke,
which I push through to him,
an inmate of the streets
I am reprieved from for now,
hidden in a seaside ghetto,
blessed by Medicare
and Medicaid
smooth sailing today
not a bothersome motherfucker
to suck the wind out of me
and lead me to drown.

THE LEAGUE OF DISTINGUISHED GENTLEMEN

It's wall to wall testosterone
underneath the eaves
of an old house
in the heart of Cambodia Town,
dried out & dope sick
alcoholic & addicted men
smoke cigarettes
& drink mud strong coffee,
listening to different songs
on their phones at the same time:
LL Cool J does battle
with Hagar era Van Halen,
but nobody wins here
in a place where the main objective
is not staying sober, going back to school
& getting a job but meeting women online
with the hope of a midnight fuck behind
the Home Depot up on Signal Hill
overlooking the entire city
as it falls prey to the sins of the night.
It's daytime here in the land of darkness,
& nobody's getting laid because
women are wise enough
not to fall for 21st century
deadbeat men scratching lottery tickets
at seven AM when the energy has

false hope, before the mosquitos fly in
& the patio turns into a ghost town.
Only the sounds of television
soap operas, The Price is Right
& the snores of men are heard,
men who all forgot that time
gave them a chance beyond
the blood stained concrete where
daydream gambles go up in smoke
& burn into dead end nightmares.

POSTER BOY FOR HILLSHIRE FARMS

my portly roommate gazed at me
from the reflection
in his mirror, when
he asked me what
I'd call his style, and I told him:
"cheese...and sausage."

KING OF COMEDY

He laid a real doozy on us
after we gave him time
during therapy to tell a joke
about a gang of ducks
who all get themselves arrested.
When questioned by the police
as to what they were doing,
each of them said *"blowing bubbles"*
until the last duck was asked his name
and he answered *"Bubbles"*
Nobody laughed at the punchline—
a woman audibly groaned, that's it.
During a coping skills themed
game of Hang-Man, the first letter
of one of the clues was "M"
and he shouted *"Masturbation!"*
Everyone looked at him sideways,
and he asked the group,
"masturbation is a healthy
coping skill, isn't it?"
to which the therapist said
"in some cases, but not
appropriate for our purposes here"
and his jaw sank low
in disappointment at her answer.
He sat in silence while
the rest of us gave out

healthy answers to healthy questions.
None of us could cope with the image
of duck fellatio quacking in our heads,
but I think I know what he did with
his free time after our session.

ENTERTAINMENT FROM THE DEAD

The people on my friend's television
in sitcom reruns from the 1960s
are high definition technicolor corpses,
the canned laughter a false joy
of dead people, the gags unfunny
and the plots cliched in teleplays
written by overpressured hacks.
I used to watch these shows
growing up, and dreamed one
day I'd be on one but now
I'm relieved not to be preserved
like an artifact to be scrutinized
by lazy couch potatoes,
imprisoned by syndication,
a ghost trapped in character.

NOT QUITE RIGHT

They decorated
a memorial tree
for a dead patient at
our mental health clinic
with bones and a skull
spattered with
fake blood
for Halloween.
When I first saw it,
I laughed and wondered
if the dead patient
would laugh
at his potentially
offensive,
macabre rise
from the dead,
and knowing him,
he probably would,
the smile of his
ghost beaming
from a demented
great beyond.

ITCHY & SCRATCHY

He's got a scab
in the middle of his forehead
that he picks at constantly.
It never heals, and
sometimes it bleeds.
The nurses put bandaids
on it, but they never stay
put and wind up clinging
to his cheek or
resting on his shoulder.
He begs for cigarettes
all the time on breaks
from group, reaching out
to the other patients
with bloody hands
they plead with him
to go wash after
they all say no,
but he doesn't listen,
sitting there with
his fingers on
his face, with
faint whimpers for
someone to give them
something else to do,
like a cigarette
or a piece of candy

to fill the hole
he is digging deep
into the saddened skin
on his forehead
until his troubled mind
is exposed to us all.

STRANGER DANGER

He has a face only a shovel
could have smashed in,
filling me in on all of the lowdown,
dirty, sinister people he claims are after him.
His own daughter put a hit out on his head
over a dispute involving a loaded revolver
and her baby daddy, but the rest of his story
always come out in whispered gibberish,
one tooth top center of his wide mouth
as he rambles on into my ear at therapy
during smoke breaks, lunch, even while
the cleaning lady mops the linoleum
of the patient lobby, where he offers me
a ride home in his beat-to-hell convertible
that he claims to have gotten "for free."
His unintelligible speech makes it difficult
to gather if he's an undiagnosed,
paranoid schizophrenic or just plain high
on some type of alleyway pharmaceutical,
but either way, the deep nicotine stained
wrinkles on his face tell me his real story,
and it casts him as my father's cellmate
at the many prisons he's served time in,
hardened by a life I can't understand
from stories of the Mongol bikers hot
on his tail to slit his throat to fears
he won't live much longer or

the phone conversations I overhear him
having, when voices scream from inside
the sweaty palms of his large claws,
a man too strange, questionable
and dangerous for me to cruise
the streets of the free world with,
because he triggers me far more
fiercely than the triggers on
any of the guns my father used
to spray the world with an ugliness
I'd rather walk home and forget.

ACROSS THE BORDERLINE

There's something in the expression
on his face that tips me off—he's triggered
by something in group, & I know it was
probably a generalization about trauma
a girl made moments before that
alienated him, made him feel unheard.
I could see it in his eyes, a tortured look
of abandonment & invalidation, an urge
to get up & explode all over the place
until the cortisol dies out, he's cooled down,
clear-headed, guilty over his actions,
ashamed. Puzzled over the specifics
in the past that gave birth to this thinking,
this feeling, this behavior, how to be rid of it.
I know all of this because I'm looking
into a mirror on the other side of the room.
We both know this pain none of the others
are even aware of, only when we have
outbursts of anger we bottle up for
the sake of being nice guys. Cross-talk
out of control, our therapist's voice
drowned out *one at a time one at a time*
but we both sit there, silent, until it's over
& we are the only ones left there, sitting
in the dark, talking about our problems.

NO TIME FOR LOSERS

We both lay here in our adjacent beds,
my roommate at the sober living and I,
his cheap old transistor radio dialed into
K-Earth 101, Queen screaming that
We Are the Champions of the World.
Both of us jobless, stabilized by a trove
of psychiatric medication, enough to
sedate an elephant, too foggy to rule
the world. My roommate shares all
of his manic delusions with me, and
I'll keep on fighting to the end to keep
my own sanity while he jabbers on
about the Russians and Boy George,
how they are tapping his phone, which
rests on his bare fat belly, rising up
and down in victory breaths, my
roommate shirtless while he waits
for his deodorant to dry so he can go
downstairs and mop the dining room
floor. While he does that, I sweep
the carpeted stairs that lead up to
our second story room to make our
landlord happy we finished our chores,
then back to a life whose soundtrack
is K-Earth, conversations surreal
paintings on the ceiling we stare at
together all day, trapped here inside
a sideshow nobody would pay to see.

STRAIGHT OUT OF CENTRAL CASTING

He's a 74-year old washed-up Howdy Doody,
wooden skin carved into wrinkles after
a lifetime of smoking, drinking and drugging.
He mumbles the obscure jokes of a demented,
red faced goon. His mustache dances
in between his nicotine yellow fingernails
while he laughs into his hands, stifled sneeze
drool rests on his chin next to a large mole,
a curly hair growing out of it an old crackwhore
bites out with her dentures at lunch. Staff sees
it, but they don't care. In group therapy, his
favorite topic is his dubious claim of having
been a tenured rocket scientist at Boeing who
designed the jetpack man used to travel to Mars.
One of many reasons why he is on strings and
doesn't pull them. You'd think a woodchipper
had gotten around to him by now, but his
ventriloquist genetics keep him upright
in a cigarillo lipped smoke cloud haze
until his long-running show is canceled.

LOW BLOW

You look
just like
Eddie Munster
with your hair
parted and greased up
like that,
Peggy said to Jose,
who gnarled his lip
and winced.
A sustained,
dreaded *nooo*
came out
of his mouth
while everyone
else laughed
that's cold
he whispered
that's cold
and Pablo nodded
like an audience
member on Oprah,
without a clue
as to what was
even going on,
because he wasn't
paying attention
and usually does

that no matter
what anyone says,
including our
therapist, who
doesn't watch T.V.

PEST

a kid
at my house
asked me
why I look tired
all of the time
and I told him
it was because
of his youth

THE ZEN MASTER OF ATLANTIC AVENUE

He sits in a busily arranged garden
devouring the parameters of
his humble, corner lot abode,
an inner city oasis hidden
among oceanside ghetto slums.
Relentless reminders of
the human condition's frailty
line every gutter, but not his,
the sidewalks are so clear
and immaculate, they enable
him to stroll barefoot
across the finely swept,
graffiti-free concrete.
I always see him while
en route to a psychiatrist's office,
startled by his spying presence
amid the thick brush and fauna,
fruits of a plant whisperer
and commonplace bodhisattva
who welcomes me into the grace
of a warm smile, and he
offers it every time I pass by,
when both of our arms shoot up
to wave a hello marinated
in innocent enthusiasm
before I continue on my quest
for the Western medicine

I was raised on alongside
white bread, cheese wiz,
Miracle Whip and deviled ham,
but someday I'll stop and see
if this wise old man prescribes
me a starting dose of his obvious
enlightenment to heal me from
the nonsense I was taught.

LAUGHING IN THE FACE OF DEATH

Her best friend had died,
and I was a failure at consoling her.
I'd lost many people to the Reaper
in recent years. I got tongue tied
and just listened to the rawness
of her grief. I handed her a tissue
and told her to let me know if there
was anything I could do. She glanced
at her phone, when she began to laugh,
drying her tears and I asked her
what was so funny. She showed me
a photograph I'd posted on social media
of me in my underwear, which chased
away her tears. She passed it
around to our fellow patients
to my protests and they laughed
so hard, the ground underneath
the floor shook like an Earthquake.
Thank you, she said. I needed that.

ANIMAL SUNRISE

I stood at the corner
of Tenth and Cherry
in the morning sun,
waiting for the smoke shop
to open up—battered,
bruised and damn near broken,
cussing quietly to myself
in languages I had not
previously known existed.
Out of the corner of my eye
I saw a German Shepherd's
shadow and got whipped
by his tail several times
as he circled around me
in excitement, which
bound me in his leash
of Lakers purple and gold.
Therapy saved my life
in that strange moment:
deep breathing,
cool and calm once
I saw that his owner
who I initially
had wanted to scream at
was a hardcore skinhead,
his face covered in
tattoos of burning skulls.

He said sorry about that.
He unwrapped me from
my chains, and I quietly
thanked him in my head
for not murdering me.
I continued to stand,
waiting, looking
at the pigeons lined up
along the telephone line,
wondering how
I was going to avoid
the path of their shit,
rotten splatters against
dangerous pavement
in an urban wild kingdom
where errands are cursed
by surprise booby traps—
kindness is a useful armor,
no matter how pissed off I get.

TAKE ME AWAY FROM THE BALL GAME

Curtis tells me the Dodgers' chances
are limited this season:
lots of naysaying disappointment,
but he's proven wrong when they defeat
the Padres in the playoffs
and Curtis celebrates with the other
dugout-heads and Big League chewers,
the rude loudmouth screams from every
living room on the block every night
drives me upstairs to read a book,
watch a movie or get so lost in thought,
I try to predict the future
or read people's minds
and I fail at both, but
my disinterest in baseball
gives me the power of being
invisible to everyone else.

BURNT TOAST

Ratgut innervisions
only fools, scoundrels
& poets can dream up
take a step forward
in the tremulous dance
of coffee mug reflection:
a weary smile, alone
in a transformative
process built out
of impatient sneers
& promises beyond
the wildest metaphor,
more dangerous
in medicinal potency
than the holiest joke
told by the biggest
wisenheimer on
planet earth—
this is the food
of gods,
& I steal a taste
whenever I can.

CLOSE ENCOUNTERS

a barefoot young woman
marched toward me
in the crosswalk at Pacific Avenue
talking to herself from the steps
of the Billie Jean King Public Library
her skin a deep bronze
& her insanity ignored
for a second of brief
irrationality on my part
her stunning beauty
a wayward distraction
until cars honked sirens
& I saw oncoming traffic,
a faceless rage of brake pedals,
our lives spared, I stumbled over
to the library steps
where a speed freak
who got ejected from
my group therapy for slugging
a blind schizophrenic man
who caught him stealing
his lunchtime soda
appeared from out of nowhere.
The X Files theme song
haunts my head whenever
he appears to me
on the streets—

a toothless,
Sasquatch meets
Where's Waldo?
meets Charles Manson
otherworldly
daylight phenomenon,
one who always asks me
for spare change
before he disappears
into extraterrestrial limits
of a crackhead unknown
beyond my imagination,
in a filthy gutter where
I sometimes nearly
get killed when I notice
the shine left in its defeat.

SHE WENT TO TAHITI

That's what she told us
whenever she came back
to outpatient after being
in patient at a local
hospital psych ward
and had to explain herself,
so she always said she had
been in Tahiti. Her devotion
to metaphysics helps me
make sense of the tragedy
of her sudden death in a
traffic collision, when she
was finally starting to find herself,
her hair cut off in a Harpo Marx
defiance and her jokes to me
about my many ridiculous
winter hats after a Christmas
in Idaho which I bet her was
nowhere near as good as Tahiti.
I stand here in the glow
of lit memorial candles
so I can tell her to say hi
to my girlfriend and my Mom
and Marlon Brando in Tahiti,
and that I'll see them again
some sunny day along exotic
shores where mad hearts
and mad minds never die.

ONE-ARMED POEM

He stands in front of you
in line at the supermarket,
slowly bagging Jack Daniels
& Marlboro Reds
at seven in the morning
with one arm, the other one
missing. The cashier waits
for you to pay for your coffee,
but you're still waiting for
the one armed man to
finish bagging his items.
He thanks you for your
patience, having to do
everything with one arm
is hard & you simply
tell him you can't imagine
before he disappears
like his arm did before him,
leaving you to wake up
& realize you haven't
lost a damn thing yet.

ROLLS-ROYCE

A portly man
decked out
in cargo shorts
& a Cheeto stained
California flag hoodie
greets me at the locked
front doors of the
Mexican supermarket
every morning
as we wait for it to open.
He always purchases
two large fresh
baked rolls &
he sighs whenever
I beat him to be first
in line at the register,
but he always beats
me home as I walk,
on a second hand
bicycle decorated
in stickers for
every punk band
in California,
plastic bakery
bag clenched
in fist against
the handlebars,

the closest thing
to a Rolls-Royce
in the whole
neighborhood.

GAS STATION CAFE

I've just butt-dialed
the ambulance company
collections agency
who's been hounding me
for months as I attempt
to shake out the last dregs
of sugar into room-
temperature coffee
brewed yesterday.
Hazelnut creamer is not
my favorite but I agree
to stir it in with lumps
of undissolved, non-dairy
powder as a faint voice
hollers my name from
inside my pocket
if I'm "ready to talk"
when I pull my phone out,
take a sip of what turns
out to be decaf and hang up.

WHEN THEY COME FOR US

We spend the remaining days of the year
watching classic episodes of *Cops*, a show
that reminds us of our ne'er-do well parents
and the list of crimes we guilted ourselves over,
a fact which made us avoid the program
when it first aired on television with
the sinister bump of its reggae theme music.
The grandparents who stepped in to raise us
studied the cases it depicted to make sense
of the mistakes their own children made,
mistakes we've come close to making
in the past handcuff us to precarious fates.
Her mother didn't come for Christmas this year,
and my father is doing time in a state prison.
Now we are left to ourselves to dip into
a mire we ran from with our college degrees
and our attempts to build new families,
to make sense of why people do what they do—
including the people who brought us into this life
only to look up and watch them break a part
an impossible pangea of flesh, blood, and bone,
psychosocial contraband scattered
across the gutter to be picked through
as our Miranda Rights are read to us
and the officers ask us what made us think
we could run from the arrested development
of bitter destinies whose chains

we managed to break free from,
but the fence was too high for us to scale.
The past got us by the feet and we turned to see
it again when it dragged us through old dirt,
our faces blurred, two question marks
cussing out the whole damn world.

RAY OF THE FUTURE

Maybe I'll visit
in the summer
next time:
the swimming pool
won't be frozen
and will inspire
sunburn eulogies
of my once pale skin.
I will have bug bites
to scratch at, hungover
and wrapped in a towel
on the back deck
staring into the
green resurrection
of the forest
beyond the backyard
of your new house,
where a playset
whispers promises
of future children
who'll call me uncle,
splash me in the face
and stand in my sun.

PUSSY POWER

My salvation began
with a wily black kitten
following me down
Vina Avenue
to 10th Street
every morning,
pawing at my feet
to command my attention:
he's adopted me, alongside
the rest of the stray cats
of the city, who've
talked me into feeding them
with any spare scratch I've got,
stopping into alleyways
to be sure they're safe—
a far more deserving charity
than the angry, desperate people
who cuss at me in every language
imaginable. These felines speak in
a purring, divine tongue of gratitude,
a feisty hairball of energy needed
at a time of world upheaval
when these little rapscallions
keep me well-fed in spirit
enough to give a good damn
about anything or anyone else.

FOOTPRINT RIVALRY

I used to think I was the only
grown adult in Southern California
who never learned how to drive a car,
condemned to walk endless pavement,
sometimes with zero destination—
until the day I saw the lanky man
with headphones on one side of the city
and then another side of the city,
walking past me with a blank face,
eyes pointed forward to nowhere.
Around the third time or so that
this happened, he began to sneer at me,
threatened by our shared claim to infamy,
honked car horns a language we could
both speak in our mutual profanity,
but we hold our harsh words whenever
we pass each other. On one occasion,
I nodded at him in acknowledgement,
and his grimace told me
these sidewalks aren't big enough
for the both of us, but we're
too disillusioned with society
and life to fight each other over it,
an unwelcome reminder
that even outsiders have to put up
with trespassing into one another's
quest to be God's lonely man.

THIS IS GOING TO TAKE
A THOUSAND YEARS

My friend says
as she warms
a hot melt glue gun
to make strands of flowers
for a display she's building
for her grandmother's birthday bash,
and it makes me think
of the scripted lines
I once repeated over and over again
when I was a child actor cast
in a Stanley Tools
Christmas television ad,
seated on Santa's lap,
asking for a socket set
and a hot melt glue gun,
and while the money I made
paid for the college
where I met my friend,
it didn't teach me
how to use
a hot melt glue gun,
making me useless to her
while she cusses and tries
to get the party decor just right,
and I stare off into space,
stuck inside of memories
while she tries to make them.

Kevin Ridgeway is the author of *Too Young to Know* (Stubborn Mule Press, 2019) and *Invasion of the Shadow People* (Luchador Press, 2022), in addition to over a dozen chapbooks and split books. His work has appeared in *Hiram Poetry Review, New York Quarterly, Paterson Literary Review, Gargoyle, Slipstream, Chiron Review, Nerve Cowboy, Heavy Feather Review, San Pedro River Review* and *Trailer Park Quarterly*, among others. A Pushcart and Best of the Net nominee, he lives and writes in Long Beach, CA.

This project was made possible, in part, by generous support from the Osage Arts Community.

Osage Arts Community provides temporary time, space and support for the creation of new artistic works in a retreat format, serving creative people of all kinds — visual artists, composers, poets, fiction and nonfiction writers. Located on a 152-acre farm in an isolated rural mountainside setting in Central Missouri and bordered by ¾ of a mile of the Gasconade River, OAC provides residencies to those working alone, as well as welcoming collaborative teams, offering living space and workspace in a country environment to emerging and mid-career artists. For more information, visit us at www.osageac.org

Osage Arts Community